Pushing and Pulling

Monica Hughes

Photographs by Mark Coote

Collins

I am pushing.

3

I am pulling.

I am pushing.

7

I am pulling.

I am pushing.

I am pulling.

Pushing and pulling

pushing

pulling

 Ideas for reading

Written by Linda Pagett B.Ed (hons), M.Ed
Lecturer and Educational Consultant

Reading objectives:
- read and understand simple sentences
- use phonic knowledge to decode regular words and read them aloud accurately
- demonstrate understanding when talking with others about what they have read

Communication and language objectives:
- follow instructions involving several ideas or actions
- express themselves effectively, showing awareness of listeners' needs
- listen attentively in a range of situations

Curriculum links: Physical Development; Knowledge and understanding of the world

High frequency words: I, am, and

Interest words: pushing, pulling

Word count: 18

Resources: a whiteboard

Build a context for reading

- Encourage the children to push their palms together as hard as they can and then, with interlocking fingers, try to pull their hands apart.

- Play 'Simon says' with a variety of push-pull commands, e.g. *Simon says pull your little finger.*

- Discuss things we push and things we pull, e.g. we push pushchairs, we pull dogs on leads.

- Walk through the book with the children, modelling turning pages in the correct order, looking at the pictures and identifying pushing and pulling activities.

- Lead a read through together using your copy, pointing to each word as you read and pausing before the words *pushing* and *pulling*, and encourage the children to use the information in the pictures to guess the word.

Understand and apply reading strategies

- Ask the group to read independently in a low voice, matching written words to spoken words. Encourage early finishers to reread to each other.

- Observe each child reading, praising and prompting good matching and use of picture cues.